For BEK, TEP, BGC, and sometimes JHH

seeds

Miriam Elisabeth Moore

Atlanta

Copyright © 2016 by Miriam Elisabeth Moore
Published by VerbalEyze Press

All rights reserved. Printed in the United States of America. No part of this book may be used or reproduced in any manner whatsoever, including Internet usage, without written permission from VerbalEyze Press except in the case of brief quotations embodied in critical articles and reviews.

Cover art by Miriam Elisabeth Moore
Edited by Kelsey Beach
ISBN: 978-1-943865-95-6

VerbalEyze Press books are available at special discounts for bulk purchases in the United States by corporations, institutions and other organizations.

For information, address VerbalEyze Press, 59 Thayer Avenue SE, Atlanta, Georgia 30315.

VerbalEyze does not participate, endorse, or have any authority or responsibility concerning private correspondence between our authors and the public. All mail addressed to authors are forwarded, but the publisher cannot, unless specifically instructed by the author, give out an address or phone number.

VerbalEyze Press
A division of VerbalEyze, Inc.
www.verbaleyze.org

Contents

Preface 1

seeds 5
danced around red 6
For You 7
this Little 8
T.E.P. 9
rain so prosy 11
would 12
snippets of beach 13
patchwork serenades 14
when I'm with you 15
beautiful everythings 16
Tuesday 17
The clouds on fire 18
Week's worth of infinity 19
sunshine muse 20
O my friend 21
Sea you 22
Eulogy lullabies 23
All she could do 24
leaving 25
watercolor sky 26
I can see better in the dark 27
when can I [please] see you again? 28
The Universe on Pause 30
September cannot come soon enough 31
sunset 32
And the silence 33
sprung 34
J.H.H. 35
Wring 36

Travel	37
Midnight	39
K.L.C.	40
Trophy	41
broken smile and hopeful allusions	42
shoulder	43
kitchen days	44
A letter to my mother on her half-birthday	45
Seasons of You	47
evaporated	48
Fall	49
Caught in the rain	50
I love it when you laugh	51
not a drumbeater: For Bethany	52
The Girl with the Wasp in her Hair	54
spring too	55
Sweet fragrance of love	56
Slice of Silence	57
breathing	58
Piece of the floor	59
Time Zones	60
Pockets of Now and Then	61
A Georgia peach in Minnesota	63
River of bees	64
spring	65
Sheets	66
a kind of sad poem about a melancholy cactus named henry who just wants love	67
New Leaf	68
sunflower seed	69

seeds

Preface

A preface should explain the purpose of a book. A preface should justify why you, lovely reader, are holding this deceased tree carcass in your hands when, in its former life, the tree could have been providing you with oxygen and, thus, your life. I have taken away the potential for life and replaced it with words. Now I am writing more words to explain why you should not resent such an action. Why are the scribbles on these pages worth your while, what will they add to your life, and will their intended addition to your life be worth the opportunity cost of the otherwise breath-providing tree? I will answer you.

    Someone I call "Pete" (but whom others call other things) once told me that poetry is the closest thing we have to the truth. I do not know what The Truth is but I do believe that the splatterings of morphemes we call poesy knock on the door of truth. Many times I am inarticulate to the point of articulation. The poetry on the following pages expresses sentiment as an inarticulate truth. My desire is that readers can bring all that *they* are to reading words that bring all that *I* am. Maybe then, after mingling about in some thoughts for a bit, readers can leave knowing perhaps more than before and feeling perhaps more than before, but changed all the same.

    Seeds is a story of change and beginnings and old and new and hope and not hope. Life is a story of change and beginnings and old and new and hope and not hope. *Seeds* is my life and everyone's life. Now this life is no longer oxygen but letters and words and phrases. I am sorry, dear tree, that you gave your life for symbols meaningless to you.

I am hopeful, dear reader, that you may find hope, life, and truth in the symbols meaningless to plant life but meaningful to *Homo sapiens*. I hope you like these words.

"How odd I can have all this inside me and to you it's just words."
–David Foster Wallace

seeds

if I had a   seed   for every time I
                    thought of you,
I could plant an endless garden.
                  and if the
    burgledeegook of the world ever hugs me too tight
I know you can hug me tighter. and it's good.
I could skipple
        down
            my garden path
ignoring the yucky roses and hurumphing the yummy
gardenias (I love gardenias) knowing it's you,
        and you,
    and always you.
I don't fear splashing through puddlewonderful glosh
                because it waters our love flowers
(and how many are yellow?).
we can hold hands if you want
    and watch paintbrush clouds up in the up there.
        while our happy seeds race each other
        under our happy toes.

danced around red

today she danced
around red,
trails of autumnal gravitation
in her wake
and blue sky reflected in her
brownleafcrunch eyes.
she smiled at yellow today
and   dipped   her toe
in more
almost red,
      praying that the warm palette
never turn to brown
           and the fallfire colors
never fade.

For You

I like it when you tell me odd facts about color perception
and your nose is a swoopy
>> ski
>> > slope
>> > > thing.
and when I look at you funny and
you look back at me funny I love you.
your hair goes like a
    floppy curtain
that gets in your eyes that are
secretly blue oh how I love you.
you lie on the floor with your secret
blue eyes shut and I'm there too
then you open your eyes and look at me
with those crinkly eyes
with a smile in them
smiling only
for me.

this Little

this Little murmurs home
but it's lost in and where?
moonlight serenade the noon.
say, little, say, the stars bleed
on our impossibility
but they bleed light.
when tasseled dresses catch
flutter and time goes so
forward and the sky is so
much and o poor
lonely earth, do the stars cry?
but how about maybe what about
happy impossibility, yes, Little?

T.E.P.

I fear dropping you on the trail behind me
like hansel and gretel crumbs to lead me home because
I have always had a home in your smile,
a home in your smile that is always an adventure.
We can go on more adventures.
We can climb mountains and paint the sky.
We can walk until we head-butt the horizon
and catch all the forevers on our fingertips.
I want to be the harmony to your life's soundtrack,
forever whispering secrets into your palm
and unlocking my heart to your eyes in a simple second.
There are so many seconds left
and so many of them to share with new people.
A light shines out of you and it hurts my eyes
when we are together because I know that one day
I will be in the dark without you to light my way.
But I know that there are many who are in the dark now
and need your light to put them back
on their hansel and gretel trails.
So I will let you go.

I will paint your smile in the sky
and send you the horizon covered in forevers.

I will hum our heartbeat melody
and I will know that at the same time
you are humming the harmony.

rain so prosy

rain so prosy
(kiss)
walk(ing) on tiptoes
i don't know
how you do (it)

how you
so ever so
(gently) refresh
and begin
(like spring)

to sigh me to
sleep and forget me
(you) grab roots
with your wee
fingers and spur stir

now it is
now, rain, now
i remember
from whence
i (come) came

would

I would smear skies of infinity across canvases of universe,
plant a forest of trees in the dark corners of my heart
where not even the sun can reach, and I would
close my eyes and surrender my fate to the wind.

I would let Chopin's nimble fingers guide me
down puddled streets and whisper me into shadows.
I would stroke wisps of alto breezes and breathe in
the warmshine caressing my face.

I would flick smiles like raindrops on you and the gardenias
while I tell the clouds about my day, showing them
how I can click my heels and paint melodies
and words in all the colors of the rainbow

I would do it all
if you would too.

snippets of beach

on the backs of polaroid pictures
scribbled with
inspired and fatigued urgency:
melting waves,
pouring sunshine,
and rainbows diving through the clouds
to grasp the
sand that felt like silk.

patchwork serenades

I am sitting to write a sonnet for the sunshine
whose mirages I mirrored
                       secretly.
You know I would pugwaddle through the murk to your
    house to see your face.
    Our symphony of patchwork serenades is infinite and
I am forever dreaming in the   six-stringed darkness
      of peaceful astronautness
                  and looking at
the clouds stuck on empty fishing hooks as
                          I throw the
                          key to the lock
into the soggy abyss of
sunshinelessness.

when I'm with you

when I'm with you the
clouds drip crayola rainbows
and I feel at home.

beautiful everythings

So many beautiful everythings we cannot see
because we are not allowed to
and even squinting will not let you see the swirling universe
that spirals around your inspired being
like a ribbon of invisibility.
And even staring unblinkingly
until you taste your tears is not long enough
for the secret lovelies to come out of their hiding places.
Because where would we be without the beautiful everythings
that push our reality to the point where it is
bursting at the seams?

Tuesday

It's always a Tuesday.
Tuesdays are unclearly nonclarity.
Tuesdays are always the ones to
dip their toes in the puddle on the side
of the street still shining from the rain
and wiggle them around, making
the mud and sediment swirl in
jubilant fractals of *what?*
Why do you do this Tuesday?
Why are you so *especially* while you
carry tornados in your back pocket?
I'll lie awake this Tuesday night,
my mind sprinting to the finish line
that is always moving, my brain
playing Musetta's Waltz on replay and wishing
everything could be more like Wednesday.

The clouds on fire

The clouds on fire
remind me to
add to the list of those who are gone,
to hold on to the sunset, and to remember the snare
drum leaves that
sang of change and newness and the future.

The clouds on fire
drip on the watercolor trees
that look like Mr. and Mrs. God
cut out the trees on the postcards
from their relatives who are
on vacation in October-land
and glued them onto a scrapbook of reality.

The clouds on fire
billow and melt like all of the existings that I know
enduring only in my memory.

Week's worth of infinity

Two weeks ago it was
a week's worth of infinity
before I would see you next.
Now, five days later, the world is in slow motion
With twelve millennia per minute,
And I'm not even waiting.
I have only a tick of tapping
and sitting and staring
and watching and wondering
And blank eyes unseeing into an
invisible space between realities
Before Friday.
And then one day before it will have been a week.
And I'm not waiting.
I am an unwilling Prufrock.
Trapped in a love song that isn't.
Wanting but not knowing what.
Feeling too much and not enough.
As the world turns past me and
behind me simultaneously,
I dream in that space
Between realities with you.

sunshine muse

I am jealous of the driftwood graveyards
and the men who light their cigars on advent wreath candles.
My piano only plays minor tunes
and my little old ladies only drive big fat trucks
now that everything is for my sunshine muse.

O my friend

(O my friend loneliness,
come back to bed.)
You call me a nihilist
But I like the smell of morning
(when I awake from my
tangerine dreams).

Sea you

When kindergarten me dreamed
About breathing under water
In calm, dry, subconsciousland,
I had no idea it was like this.
Everything melts away like ice
In the first sigh of spring
And I get lost in the black abyss.
The waves of warm homeliness
Murmur me to sleep
As they rock me
In the underwater heaven.

Eulogy lullabies

When there couldn't be
possibly more
and then
you do.

Summer eulogy lullabies
I wish
I could wisp
To spring hums.

All she could do

All she could do was
Sit on the edge,
Close her eyes,
Rest her head in her hands,
And count her breaths.
All she could do was
Paddle in memories,
Escape to purple dreams,
Clench her jaw,
And paint on a smile.
All she could do was
Everything she could do
To make her forget
That you never said goodbye.

leaving

It always felt like time was moving slowly,
creeping as leisurely as possible,
like it was made out of peanut butter,
like God was watching the
claymation world in stop motion.
Until you told me you were leaving
and then God pressed fast forward.
I say "I'll see you soon then"
but my empty suitcase lying on the floor disagrees.

watercolor sky

all of the togethers were already asleep when
he hid in the laundry room
with his sea glass eyes
to escape the whispers and
the melting of the
watercolor sky

I can see better in the dark

The fire of burning bridges stings my face
But I can see better in the dark.
Spindly arms of aloneness are reaching out to me
So I close my eyes,
Take a deep breath,
And fall into their embrace.

when can I [please] see you again?

I'm afraid I'll forget what you feel like
and that my muscle memory
will be lost in dying synapses.

I don't want my fingertips to forget you,
to go limp at my sides,
helpless and lost for a purpose.

Our tragic inevitability is broken
and when I looked ahead all I saw
were picture frames of *retrospective you.*

Since I read you the gory bits
of scary shark books
in the back of math class

and laid out new beginnings
with new bowls of morning cheerios,
you have been mine.

You were captured in words
but now I see you slipping away. So
all I want to know is howhaveyoubeen?

and when can I [please] see you again?

The Universe on Pause

Snow like feathers
frozen in time in the wind,
wondering, wandering wings,
floating, flying, downy down to the
muffle-world suppressed into peace.

September cannot come soon enough

The wind used to carry me
piggyback down the street.
And the sun used to hug me
and smile into my eyes.
Now suddenly the wind is gone
And the stillness steals my breath
as it takes years
to walk down the street
with my feet trying to grow roots wherever I step.
The sun hides her smile
behind the clouds that
Seep into my skin and squeeze through my ears
and nose
and mouth
until all I can see is the foggy reality
that you are gone.
June echoes the truth that
September cannot come soon enough.

sunset

and we chased the moon across the sky
until the sun kissed the sea
goodnight

And the silence

You had been gone
and you were going to be gone some more.
But all the goneness flew away
when she saw you at her door that morning.
You held her and suffocated her goodbyes,
leaving only smiles.
You were there and she was there
and you floated together in the silence,
bodies braided. She thought that
the goodbyes would be gone forever
as the silence embraced you.
The bright inside her burned even brighter
but then you were gone again.
That night she stood in the shower
letting the water wash you away
down the drain. The silence pitied her.
she slept your smell out of her bed
as the silence rocked her to sleep.
You had been gone
and you were going to be gone some more.

sprung

april showers are
flurries that imprison
may flowers in
icesoil with no
sweaters or spring

and the sun wears
cumulonimbus to
cushion the truth
that here, the new
and the sprouts wait

O they wait for a while
while I hail the budtime
which is bedtime for
snow when the hail
will give way to hello

J.H.H.

You are lost in an echo
And I am floating face down in sunshine.
You were my world
And now I am on the other side of it.

Wring

I wring the remaining truth out of my heart
and into your palms.
I sigh as the feelings of
    over
          and
                done
                      whisper me into silence.

Travel

A year before
two months from now
I begged for september
and counted counted
footsteps and minutes
to your face to my home.
But it's now and september
was not as *september*
as I wanted. For leaves
turned brown and died
in my time zone and
the trees forgot them
like I forgot you.
Now the trees are
not naked and not alone
and I cannot see the sky
through their starving arms.
The sky was too much
muchness in my time zone
and my jetlag was worth
your face and my home.
But the jetlag hisses sleep

in my brainstem and reminds
me that my name is "was"
while I count clockticktocks
dragging themselves through
time and space like oil from a
cast iron pan a day late.

Midnight

Underneath appendages
sighing in their sleep
In the perfect darkness
where the night things creep

K.L.C.

I have to share you with the
other playgrounders because
You have to help other playgrounders
become who they will be.

I will remember you like
glass remembers steam.
Imprinted with you-ness
Though the *you* part is gone.

I will miss you for every little
infinity that you are away
and I will love you for every huge
infinity that I live.

Trophy

faceless bodies
trying so hard to have faces
to pull stringy blonde hair back from.
reciting beth henley scripts
instead of conversation
as they sip their bitter
low-cal protein sludge through their
lipsticked frowns.

broken smile and hopeful allusions

that girl with the broken smile
and the hopeful allusions has far away eyes.
the mournful twinkling is slowly dimming.
she is far away and melting.
someone will make it okay because
someone has a toolbox to fix her broken smile.
and someone will be the muse
that puts the light back in her eyes.

shoulder

I remember times when you
used to smile
but now l I have left are
      distorted and
            fuzzy sensory impressions
of times filled with unconscious joy and

                         snapshots
of holding each other in the kitchen
        as your tears
                dripped
                    down my shoulder.

fate has claws sharp as knives
and tears are lemon juice in the scars.

kitchen days

I want to return to those kitchen days
when god was real
and people stayed

A letter to my mother on her half-birthday

I was always in love with
The idea of escapism and
Desanctifying the sacred home
But O how I miss harmonizing
With the teakettle and you.

My life, the ballad-anthem,
Has footnotes where I added
Your name and susurrations
Of biscuit making. Three
Tablespoons of shortening.

I am taller than you now but you
Will forever be closer to the sky
And my head will forever be
In the clouds. Time and space can
Never touch those kinds of things.

Sometimes we do not notice
How many truths we heard
And ignored back in the back-then.
I realize that you were always right
While I was an eighth note behind.

The eighth notes of *almost*
Tickle my toes like you used to
And I finally like my name and
Half-sweet, half-unsweet iced tea
Because I'm half you and I like it.

Seasons of You

You smelled like Autumn,
Snuggled like Winter,
Smiled like Spring,
And like Summer, you were gone too soon.

evaporated

Drives up to the railroads crossing with no tracks,
Rolls down the windows to smell the air,
hoping that it is the same air that
ladled inspiration from the emptied blue sky
filled with evaporated wonder and humility.
Loves so pointlessly and poetically and gratefully.

Fall

He said he liked fall
because the leaves changed. He thought
change was exciting.

Caught in the rain

Sometimes it is good to get caught in the rain,
to look at the weeping sky because
beyond the clouds is the universe
where there are infinities of infinities
of possibilities and inspirations.
You found out today that you only want things
you can't have. But the rain and the dew
and the silence you can have.
And they remind you that it will be okay.
The rain will whisper sweet everythings in your ears
even when your mind seems too loud
because it is never too loud for the rain's whispers.

I love it when you laugh

I love it when you laugh.
You close your skyeyes and
throw your head back like
you want the clouds to join in too.
Then we are alone together in
our laughter realm of happiness.
We don't notice that the world
is staring at us with eyebrows raised
until we tumble back into reality
and I try to sing "You Light Up My Life"
through my eyes but by that time
you have already looked away
so I wait until the next time we return.

not a drumbeater: For Bethany

they said She was
(blonde)
but i said she (was
light)
and more sunshine
than He,

for the drumbeaters
are parading
aroundroundround
her lone hill where
she sends messages
(in bottles) to the sky.

andbutwhile her
skysun fingers
kiss piano keys
like dew drops on
petals (orwhathaveyou)
the drumbeaters listen.

(O listen)
ye drumbeaters!
(O listen) ye clouds!

by and by (o by
the by) soon,
you will grasp.

see the answers
like birds stretched
on invisible zephyr.
now drumbeaters
and He's, (the lightyears
are seconds) to we.

dear you are dearly
are sunblonde and good
(and i follow your light)
where the sky and you stood.

The Girl with the Wasp in her Hair

the girl with the wasp in her hair walked home
sunlight feeling like rain
with tears threatening to blossom
like the daffodils she saw by the road.
the girl with the wasp in her hair squinted her eyes at the sky
daring the sun to stare back.

spring too

O springy spring,
you ritual [birthing spring]
squishy squash away.
i am a dusttodust
and you are a puddle.

Sweet fragrance of love

Sweet fragrance of love,
Hold me tight
With triangles of desert
And soft sighs of
Content

Slice of Silence

I love to do nothing with you.
When we squidge-squodge together
And breathe each other's breaths,
Heartbeats syncopated.
Cut a piece of that silence for me now,
A big slice for us to share.

breathing

I get home and
I still smell like you.
Every exhale
breaks my heart
because
with every inhale
you are here with me.

Piece of the floor

On the precipice of doubt,
She carries around a piece of the floor.

"I woke up with a piece of the floor on me.
He brought more *world* to my world," says she.

O carnivorous death,
I have memorized your lipstick stain.

"I woke up with a piece of the floor on me.
He took world away from my world," says she.

Time Zones

Nowaday in the days,
(every moment or two,)
I forget that we live
in different time zones.

That I live in your past
(, which I know to be true)
and you live in my future
(where I will wait for you).

Pockets of Now and Then

"Here and there, in cold pockets
Of remembrance, whispers out of time."
Wandering through the *now*, I look up to find you
Seeping through the cracks of the past.
Some days, as I plod on
Through my winter,
I smell a smell that throws me into *before*
And my neurons cling to each other
Lest the memory fade.
Rain washed you away
And evaporated you up into the sky corners.
Sometimes I think you call to me
But your voice ricochets against the clouds,
Trapping itself in dark, locked passages
Of evaporated dreams and *woulds*.
They say my heart strengthens
But my will weakens
And a deep sigh will send me
Down the fire escape to the *then*.
The *now* is crumbling and the whispers of antiquity
Carve their way in,
Drumming the echoes of you into my ears.

My empty suitcase had a cavernous mouth
And I didn't want to feed it.
But I keep my eyes open. For
Occasionally I find a warm pocket of
See you again.

A Georgia peach in Minnesota

Where has all the sweet tea gone?
And why do these peaches say *California*?

I despise the coarse grains of sugar
Littering the bottom of my glass
Under the jingling ice cubes
Who are floating nonchalantly like nothing is wrong.

But everything is wrong.
Because no sugar is dissolving.

I caress the comforting fuzz of the peach.
I breathe in the stickysweet smell
And let the curvy fruitmusic wash over me
As I tell the peach stories of home.

You will never know rain, my Californian friend.
And you will never taste as good as Georgia.

River of bees

"In a dream I returned
To the river of bees."
I dipped my toe in its
Bumbling waves of life.
I glided up the honeycomb
Branches of oaks
And watched the purple
Sky bleed.
Drips of sunset mixed
With swirling wings
And secrets,
Reflecting into my eyes.
Awake, I return
To the dry riverbed,
Sit in the cracked dirt,
And wait to visit
My technicolor dream.

spring

my dear friend spring,
you are crisp are beginning are fresh are forget-me-nots.
my door is ever unlocked to you and
springtime is for you and me
and the new dew of tomorrow.
you dip your paintbrush in sparkling puddles
and throw rainclouds to the atmosphere,
pelting handfuls of fluff into the upthere
so the blossomblooms can harmonize
with your sweet song of
wonder and new.
you will paint my insides with flutters,
fill me with bubble-eyed mornings,
and we will float into your helium sky together.
we can   skipple   around the barefoot kisses,
music drip drop soaring
from our eyes
when our mouths are not enough.
there is too much vivid and world
in the springworld
for you keep budding and dancing and promising me
that it will not be long until
you tickle my eyelids
and I see you next.

Sheets

I live in echoes of your shadow.
She said hell is murky
But it's crystal clear.
I changed the sheets
So I wouldn't smell
That you are gone
And that all the iloveyous
Will never make you stay.

a kind of sad poem about a melancholy cactus named henry who just wants love

evolution, my sworn enemy,
you linger here still.
you curse me with spikes
and "it'sforyourowngood"
but you don't know what I want.

New Leaf

The fires of dawn
Do not shake
My new leaf new.
O tell me the truth
About the autumnfall
And the whispercrunches
That cover the ground.

sunflower seed

You are me, seed
and the world will soon be suns.
I see your bumps, lips, and scritchy scratches
but underneath your shell
is soft.
Your smooth-rough chrysalis
holds you fast so
nobody knows that you are vulnerable.
O vulnerable, gentle, wee, young seed,
the world will soon be suns.
The rain will come
and you can close your eyes.
The sky will shine a loud shimmer on you
and then there you can listen to the skysong.
You are potential my seed, my me
and the world will soon be suns.
The pumpkin seeds laugh
as they are bigger than you
but the clouds will be your pillows soon.

We are littles my dear,
proper littles, indeed

for who ever thought beauty
could come from a seed?

But don't you worry my wee seed, my me,
for the world will soon be suns.

Miriam Elisabeth Moore is originally from Atlanta, Georgia, but she is also from all the many other places she and her family cuddled cats, read books, drank tea, and called home. Such homes include: Southern Pines, North Carolina; Louisville, Kentucky; Hamden, Connecticut; and Bangalore, India.

Miriam currently lives in St. Paul, Minnesota where she studies English at Macalester College and does fun things like making messes with her watercolors, crocheting hats for her friends, singing show tunes in libraries, and quoting Kurt Vonnegut to strangers in tea shops.

VERBALEYZE
Press

Empowering young writers to say, **"I am my scholarship!"**

Open call for submissions to the *Young Writers Anthology*!

See your work in print!

        Become a published writer!

                Earn royalites that can help you pay for college!

VerbalEyze Press is accepting submissions from young adult writers, ages 13 to 22, in any of the following genres:

- poetry
- short story
- song writing
- play writing
- graphic novel
- creative non-fiction

For submission details, visit
www.verbaleyze.org

VerbalEyze serves to foster, promote and support the development and professional growth of emerging young writers.

VerbalEyze Writers Cooperative

VerbalEyze is a nonprofit organization whose mission is to foster, promote and support the development and professional growth of emerging young writers.

The Young Writers Chapbook Series is published as a service of VerbalEyze in furtherance of its goal to provide young writers with access to publishing opportunities that they otherwise would not have.

Fifty percent of the proceeds received from the sale of the Young Writers Chapbook Series are paid to the authors in the form of scholarships to help them advance in their post-secondary education.

For more information about VerbalEyze and how you can become involved in its work with young writers, visit www.verbaleyze.org.